Giraffe

Also by Stanley Plumly

In the Outer Dark

Giraffe

Poems by Stanley Plumly

Louisiana State University Press
Baton Rouge 1973

ISBN 0–8071–0065–X
Library of Congress Catalog Card Number 73–83910

Manufactured in the United States of America
Printed by Braun-Brumfield, Inc., Ann Arbor, Michigan
Designed by Albert R. Crochet

Some of these poems first appeared in the following magazines: *Greenfield Review, Gulfstream, Iowa Review, Lillabulero, New American Review, New Letters, New Yorker, Northwest Review, Partisan Review, Poetry Northwest, Salmagundi, Shenandoah, Southern Review, Striver's Row, Sumac,* and *Vanderbilt Poetry Review.*

"Walking Out" and "Giraffe" appeared in the *New Yorker.*

"With Weather" first appeared in the chapbook, *How the Plains Indians Got Horses,* Best Cellar Press.

I would like to thank Ohio University's Baker Fund Award Committee and Mr. Edwin Kennedy, whose financial assistance made the completion of this book possible. Thanks also to Wayne Dodd.

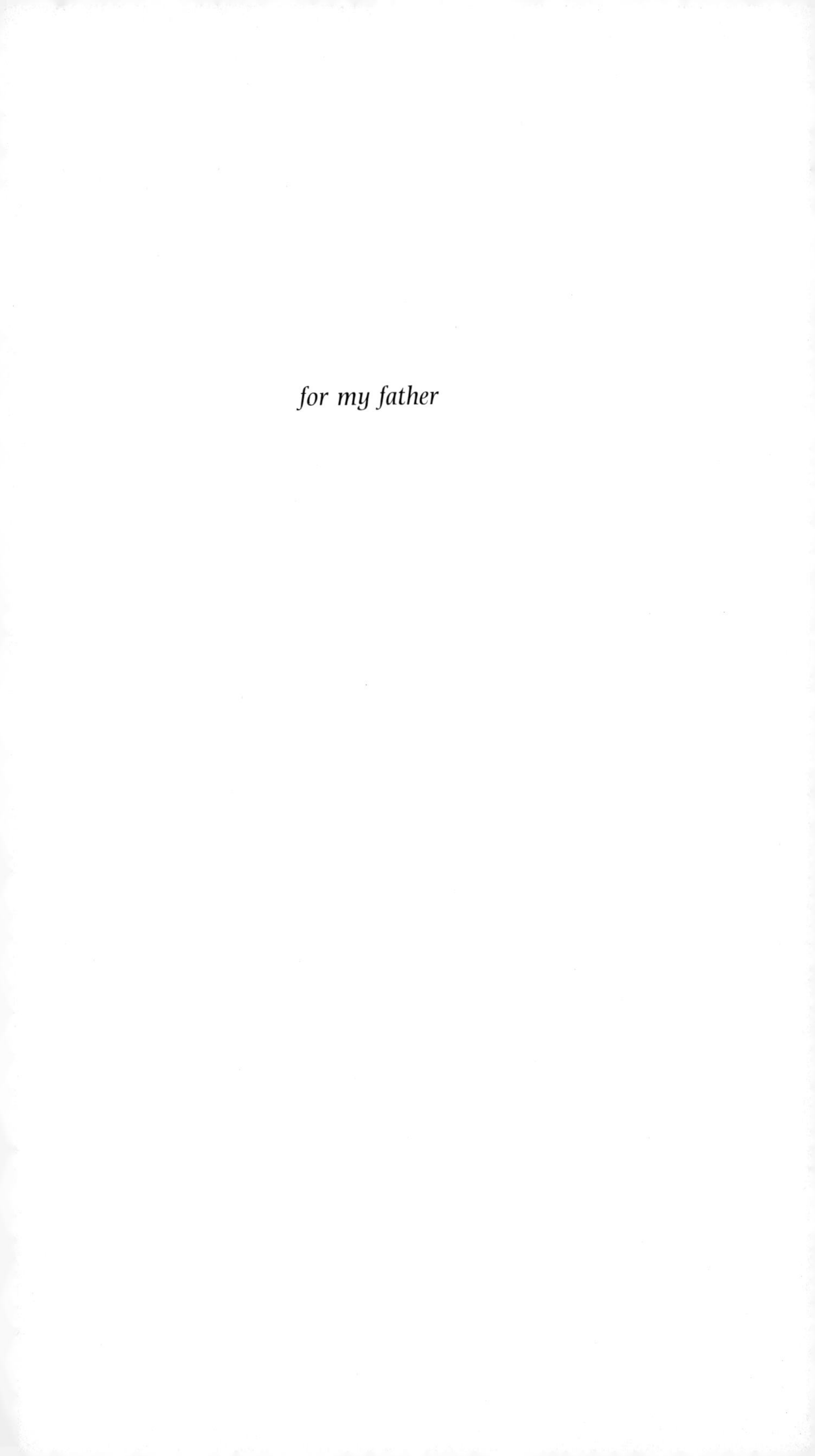

for my father

"Your Excellency does well to look at the Hyena," said he. "It is a great thing to have got a Hyena to Hamburg, where there has never been one till now. All Hyenas, you know, are hermaphrodites, and in Africa, where they come from, on a full-moon night they will meet and join in a ring of copulation wherein each individual takes the double part of male and female. Did you know that?

"No," said Count Schimmelmann with a slight movement of disgust.

"Do you consider now, your Excellency," said the showman, "that it should be, on account of this fact, harder to a Hyena than to other animals to be shut up by itself in a cage? Would he feel a double want, or is he, because he unites in himself the complementary qualities of creation, satisfied in himself, and in harmony? In other words, since we are all prisoners in life, are we happier, or more miserable, the more talents we possess?"

—Isak Dinesen
Out of Africa

Contents

Giraffe

Heron

Horse

Giraffe

Since England Is an Island

We shall not get any better
no matter how long we live.

We shall improve the makeup
of clocks, our gestures,
the pair of pants the years made fit,
my hand between your legs—

finally a place for it—
the schedule of events,
the arrival and departure of the next time
anything happens,

new money or the coins
that are never spent,
and what we can afford of our affections,
and kissing the mirror,

and you are someone else besides me,
and your left foot is childish
and falling behind
on the circle of the schedule of events,

but no matter how long we live
on the island, no one
is coming, no one is coming.

Walking Out

I would walk out of this flesh,
leave the whole body of my bones.
If I could I would undress utterly.

I would be silence: Even the sleeves
of my best coat would not know me.
I would write my name in cold blood

by a candle whose flame would fire
air, breath, everything, including paper.
I would be totally absent from myself,

from thought of myself; I would forget
myself entirely. I would go out only
at night, naked and perpetually catching

cold, and in fear of footprints, walk
on my hands. They would think *five-toed bird*
and at the edge of water imagine flight.

But I would still be walking, if I could,
out of body, leaving behind, in a wake
of absence, clothes, fingerprints, words.

Giraffe

The only head in the sky.
Buoyed like a bird's,
on bird legs too.
Moves in the slowmotion
of a ride
across the longlegged miles
of the same place.
Grazes in trees.
Bends like a bow
over water
in a shy sort of
spreadeagle.
Embarrassed by
such vulnerability,
often trembles, gathering
together
in a single moment
the whole loose
fragment of body
before the run downwind.
Will stand still
in a camouflage of kind
in a rare daylight
for hours,
the leaves spilling
one break of sun
into another,
listening to the lions.

Will, when dark comes
and the fields open
until there are
no fields,
turn in the length
of light
toward some calm
still part of a tree's
new shadow, part of the moon.
Will stand all night
so tall
the sun will rise.

Jarrell

1914–1965

I was twenty-five and had the gun
cocked dry in my dry mouth.
My head was full of traffic and Chekhov.

The dream said *this is too serious,*
a man about to walk out of his shadow
into the speed of light;

think of something else,
the next thing, a man at a table,
the page of his poem filling up,

think of something:
but I could remember only the road,
the open end, the loose fragment of lights

rising in a mass, like a star too close,
the dark piled up behind.
Dream said again *too serious,*

a man walking out of himself on a road at dawn.
A man saying out loud, I give you back this
gift, having already put it down.

Versions of Water

We know water,

that to die
is to drown.

We listen as the ear records each ocean.
We hear that sonar at the ocean floor.

*

A man in the middle of some sargasso sea
has no choice but to walk.

He will learn sooner or later
that water is the matter.

*

The fisherman stood
in his boat as if it were a shoe . . .

this single step—and
we are standing on fishes.

*

And the blue whale grazed for hours,
remembering the meadow.

The birds that grazed on his back
came to believe in the quixotic cycles
of islands.

*

The rain lasted all winter.
We kept thinking snow,

snow in the trees, our eyes,
the fields filling up,
we could hold it in both hands,

and although it fell slower
and larger, like flowers . . .

*

I was afraid of water
so they threw me in,

without oar, rudder, anything
but myself to go by.

I was the third time learning.

*

Just so: the man drowning,

the long fall through himself,
the time it takes to remember.

*

The language of the Navaho
will not admit
to the indignity of man.

Even in Arizona
the man did not drown;
the water came up to get him.

At Hub's Farm, May

The sky: my mind white with it.
Not what I thought, certainly not what
I wanted: even that Indian pony,
his body mapping an earth,
lies down in the rain,
in the middle of his pasture,
the shy half-moon
of his head
tucked into the dark
of one shoulder—
no thought except green.

I've been here three days,
sun gray up, sun gray down.
I wanted country weather.
My Quaker uncle still works
these Ohio hills at the ass end
of a plowhorse.
It's safer, he says, with an animal:
no tilt, no chance
of turning over.
No dry-spell, wind-warp,
or wash-out either: the wild pony his luck.

Buckeye

My father came to Ohio
the year the war ended.

There were four of us,
pinched in with possessions,
in a '29 Ford sedan.

You had to wind it up
and even then it farted
& spat back.
Five times it wanted to break my bony arm.

Mother sat in the backseat with my sister.
My father drove like a soldier
home from the front.
I was six and crazy
to be killed.

We drove all that first day until after dark,
Ohio being north of the way things were.

Still in Ohio

We start out in the same room
in the same hospital, now a house,
in Barnesville, Ohio.
Almost at the same time,
twenty-three years apart.
You grow up there, farm boy,
live there too long.
Your heart becomes muscle-
bound from work.
Your father is a hammer.
You hate him as you love your mother.
There is never enough.
You become a witness.
There are terrible things being said.
A long nail driven vertically through the body.
The sun on your mother's face
worries her into the ground.
When I come home.
Then you are my mother and father,
twin hammers. I grow up
and live there too long.
I marry you over
and over and over.
The heart becomes musclebound.
In the room where I make my wife
my son, still in Ohio,
you lie down.

With Weather

All day you watch the frost flare
into each dark part of the star.
The cold is like glass on your skin.
You know if you sit here long enough
how brittle the body becomes.
Even the light is on two sides.
But you sit in the sun half, half sun,
the lie in your lap, filling your face.
You're like a man in love with something—
some word, a gesture, the one line of light
among some trees, a man in a chair
watching it snow. You could get up
and walk the house or go outside.
You could move to a warmer window.
You could move to the middle of the room.
You could get up and turn on the light.
You could sit here the rest of your life.

Dreamsong

I was in the middle of the way,
  with the lights on
and the dark side rising.

I was kneeling, no traffic,
  I had the river
under me; I believed in what

I wanted. I wanted to die.
  I wanted the whole
day. So I rocked back and forth,

as in the cradle of myself, until my body
  let me. Then I rose
and walked the water, like a son.

1.7.72

Karate

If I could chop wood,
if I could just cut through
this furniture,

the paraphernalia
of blocks
and stacks of boards,
wedged and
piled
head-high,

if I could break the back
of a single two-by-four,

if the Japanese instructor would only
lay his little building
of bricks
in front of me,

if I could only drive nails
deep into the hard rose of the wood.

Four Lines in Lieu of a Poem

My father, the good Indian.
He sleeps on a door.

At night, just thinking of him,
the lumber flies at my forehead.

One Line of Light

Six across. The windows give away
everything. Some nights
I'm the only one up
in Athens, Ohio,
all the lights on,
the music loud enough
to leak, like water,
out of every seam,
each soft spot.

I think of my house as a ship
lit up like a birthday.
I walk around inside it
with the page of a poem—
the day's log,
the night's psalm.
The dark is my ocean.
I know the water's rising
in the next town.

for Bill Matthews

Woods Lake

From here, high side of the hill,
black duck or loon,
shaking its blue body loose
of the pale abstract of water
rising from water, comes at last
alive at the treelevel of light
and is paralytic that moment
that the eye dances too.

Later, in full dark, the eye will imagine
a bird wagging the black flame
of itself until everything
around it is still.
Even the eye stay shut.
Bird may then go out or burn clear
for a moment in the damp lake air,
the last thing to be thought.

The One Morning of the Month When It Rains

The clumsy children should be dancing on the lawn
or the women without underwear;

there should be barns at the edge of town
and one light in the kitchen window—

even the streetlights should come on
and the silence of water falling the only silence;

there will be the early traffic having the dream of
  countermotion,
and the sign at the city limits which says Come Back;
  but mostly

it's still dark, it's still dark the first man after dawn
  should shout,
running the sopping street toward an open field.

Heron

Fungo

From pitch and catch
to this:
sometimes I feel I've waited
whole days, and only now
in the clarity
of any evening,
both our faces filled with the hours,
have you come to me
as from the other side
of something—grief, moonpiece,
a small clock of the single,
fixed star—to lie in this room
with me all night,
perhaps a day,
and nothing between us.

*

(The summer of nineteen sixty, more than once,
I drove all the way to the end of Long Island
to watch the whales.
Even eleven years ago
I waited and waited, but never saw one.

They should have loped
like great attenuated waves
in the animal waters
just off shore, just close enough
I could have watched
the one body
leave,
enter the other.)

*

Tonight the lighthouse scatters the light like snow
over the ocean

as I push out, cloud and oar,
over the dream of your pale body.
I have no hands for this:
they do not perform
miracles,
like fish out of water.

My body falls apart, layer after layer,
inside itself
like the underwater demolition of a fish.

I turn over and over
and what do I see but your forehead
fingerprinted like an underfin.

*

I want to come to you from a distance
of light years,
from the blind side,
as if this moment
were in perpetual motion.
I want you to come to me from the distance of those waters
that just make shore—
the light in the lighthouse filling you out like a moon.

In this one room
where I turn to you
in the dark,
lights in the shallow water on the wall
above us, I want nothing
empty.

Heron

1
You still sometimes sleep
inside that great bird,
flopped out,
one wing tucked,
the other slightly broken over my back.
You still fall asleep before I do.
You still wake up
in tears.

You have what is called *thin skin:*
if I put my ear to it
I can hear the wingbeat in your heart.
I can only imagine
how far down those long flights go.

2
Last night in my dream
about the heron
I stood at the edge
of water with a handful
of stones.
I was twelve, I think.
The heron perfect, still, kneedeep,
looking at himself.

Once he lifted his wings
in a mockery of flight.
For a moment I was inside you;
I could hear the heart.
I had stones in my hands.

Light

One wife enters from nowhere
to perform the laying-on of hands.
Now you know what it is to be touched.

Your whole body is in light, as to be understood.

The woman walking from the end
of the hallway has said nothing
since she began. She is also your wife.

She is crying. She is like your body repeated.

The wife of the doors, the woman of rooms.
She is the third person. The small moons
of her hands: how they bring you back

from whatever dark to whatever body is.

Pull of the Earth

A man lies down to sleep,
to let go of the day,
and however he turns,
whatever his body believes,

he feels the earth fall away
and the eye, even in dream,
follow the perfect curve,
and though for the while

the dream may let him go,
still the day comes back
each infinitely slow step
of the way from dark.

And if in sleep I sometimes
reach for you, across
whatever distances
we dream, across the distance

I am dreaming now,
against silence
and the body's fear of falling,
if I reach across this space—

barely the width of one of us—
and you turn to me,
your full face pale
and perfect as a moon,

dream or real, as the blind
know braille, I follow
that face, its body,
and hold what I can.

Three Wives

Table and chair.
This is no marriage
but an arrangement.

Your first wife was the daughter
of a man who built houses.
Each room left you emptier.

The second stood in the middle
of rooms, auditoriums, fields
and took her name, over and over, in vain.

The third had to be tracked down
in snow, like a small animal
suddenly run out of room.

Now she sits all day at her desk
like Emily Dickinson,
pure with poems.

Under Cows

We milk the moon, or—

having lain inside you
for the duration,

some war in asia
our own animal:

against you my brilliant body
breaking down, stone
by precious stone,

into this small, final star,

while overhead colossal
Taurus creams his
favorite cow:

I say there are nations
in us breaking apart
& in our sky

whole continents reforming.
The signs are right.
This bull among the febrile china

loves you. If just once more
I milk your body with this needlepoint . . .

So Having Risen Early, This Poem

Without sleep (and nearly four in the morning),
with the birdtapping of her hand, she has turned

to me out of a woman's fear, afraid to touch me awake.
For hours, in some dream, I have felt her body

move in the hollow of itself, as if sleep
were some shape to be fitted into.

Now I turn out of the slow dream of her
to find her face pressed like the new moon

of a coin against that other surface
which sleep, even dreams, sometimes denies us.

Mile of the Animal

You have the distance.

Not simply in length of leg
or arm or the subtler length
of a finger, nor in the size
of your shoe, nor ring-size,
nor the line around your wrist;

not simply in the silence ot distance
between lips or legs, even breasts,

nor in the shape any distance
becomes (kneecap, elbow, ankle),
and though light fall five thousand
two hundred and eighty feet
in your eyes, not simply that distance.

Your blood runs for miles.
Every muscle, vein, conduit
paces itself toward its perfect
point of departure. Flesh
& bone: the dream's light-year.

But you have the distance beyond body.

Your mind throws down its perfect shadow
at your feet. You begin to walk
away from yourself, not simply out of dark.

After the Tzeltal

the man opened his eyes
and saw that he was below the earth
in the presence of the lord
of death
and rose from his waking
and walked up to the lord
and the lord said
to him 'if you wish
to see your wife
go on until you reach a river
there on its banks you will find
a horse
bring it to me'

Some nights you put
your whole head in my hands
and tell me you want to die.
If you love me, I say, love me.
Loving despair, you cry.

the man obeyed
and found the river
but saw no horse
only women washing their hair
and clothes
he looked and looked
but found no horse
and returned to the lord
and the lord
said 'go to the river again
and ask each one of the women
if she is a horse

the woman who says yes
will be your wife
tie the horse well
and bring it to me'

And the nights you put
your head in my hands
and tell me you want to die,
love me, I say, if you love me.
Loving despair, you cry.

the man returned to the river
and asked each one
until he found the woman
who said she was a horse
and began to lead her
into the presence of the lord of death
and the horse said to him
'I am your wife
I know who you are'
and passing a well
where a big fire was burning
said 'I am afraid
see those bones
in the presence of the fire
I go to the river daily
bear wood and water to the well
burn down my body'
and when they came to the lord
of death he said
to the man
'so this is your wife
the woman of the well'

And the nights you put
your head in my hands
and tell me you want to die,
I say, love me, if you love me,
if loving despair, you cry.

Horse

The Sleep-Horse

Sometimes, at pasture, in nothing
but daylight,
it even looks like a horse.

Or it stands there like tremendous furniture,
like an engine at idle,
without wings,
without the great gill,
no horn at the center of its forehead—
only a girl's good legs,
all four, shoulders,
and a body with the skill
of a shark's.

Or it floats in the midair
above your body,
moon and snowfall,
weight and pull.
Or lies down in the middle of the floor,
stone cold.

And now it circles the bed
like a hurt animal,
now it stands outside, at the window.

Now it runs in
and out of the room
on fire,
the room on fire—

now it puts its head against the wall.

Now, having stood all night in your sleep,
its long face glowing
in the air at the bed's dark side,
it starts to rock back
and forth
in the stall of itself,
nodding in pain.

By Heart

In my dream I see you
dressed out on a table,
filled with the clinician's blue light—

your face in a moon above
your body, your white arms crossed
like bones against your chest.

This is always like a memory.
And, Father, I know you know
these lines by heart.

In every sleep I dream your death.
I lie down and you lie with me.
In every room this is still

your house, your history.
And if in the morning I rise
like a ghost, outside it is still

winter and sun bright, and snow
like the memory of a long rain.

Insomnia

You could be sleepless two days running
and on the third
rise in a dawn
still dark with absence, again
with only the shadow of a sleep,
witness to your own watch,
out of bed now,
walking out of sleeplessness
to the first window with light,
and in the eye that will not shut
but will not now quite open
see, having dreamed it,
some shape of yourself at the center of the sun,
wings spread,
the body rising from fire,
from body, from infinite dead weight,
lifting to life the whole new day,
to be burned alive till dark.

How the Plains Indians Got Horses

for Two Skies, a chief of the Humanos, a Texas tribe

1
If dogs had been your sole stock in trade
and during dry season
you had had to strap
your whole household
to a travio
to be dragged across the backside of a desert,
barely a foot from
bare earth, through scrub-brush,
mesquite, scab-cactus,
at each rest your two red feet
begging to be walked out of—

and sick of the whining and fleas
and meat-eating hunger (this animal
that will eat its own excrement
and urinates constantly)

and sometimes making only ten miles a day—

if on that sixth in a succession of the worst
you saw one, for the first time,
looking hornless and man-tall
at the shoulder,
perhaps fifty, a hundred yards off,
deep in its own peace,
taking water
in a deep, green place,
and you by now tasting yourself,
you too might let the dogs go

against air,
horseflesh,
the run of the arrow.

2
And you might wonder,

having hauled down
so much of something new,
gutted and cut up and stinking in the fire,
by what four-legged power does a god move?—

You, who on hands and knees
have imagined the animal,
hooted and tied blind in the dark,
ridden the buffalo back from death,
eaten dogs as dogs eat,
and now this tall one,
this tall dog . . .

3
And the next one?
Would you get down on all fours
and paw
at your shadow?
Would you run with dogs?
Would you have two legs and land
like an island around you?

Imagine you have taken this flesh into your own,
have arranged the bones,
have waited.

And thought there could be no two of this one.
That you should starve and sleep with dogs
and the next day rise as you were
and rise the day after that
to look again for water,
to find in each step the weight of the next
and the next until you are followed
or standing still,
this footpath of your fathers.

4

Then see one, again,
at evening, in half light,
still looking like itself
but lying down,
without legs or size,
the head too small and turning,
slightly adrift the body—
after three days as if in search,
two dogs dead,
two feet, two legs . . .

And rest.
And know that come morning
you will kill what is left of the dogs
and follow it and run with it
until it lies down again

5

and tie its four legs together
or later let it stand tethered
and in all its silence not even touch it,
seeing it is only what it is,

and you with nothing with you
but yourself
and the dry hunger of the miles since the first one
stood as in sleep
or so alone it seemed born that moment,
in that place,

and that you will rise from your body
as from the ground
onto this other, second of itself, horse
and rider.

The Slaughterhouse Emotion

You stall. You turn
around, whitefaced, lowing
as if to paw

the little ground
in front of you.
Everywhere you turn

you take up room.
You were like a bull
in your body,

a muscle of the mad
animal anger
of the man who turns

now, all his soft flesh
falling. And now it moves
like clockwork

in your head.
You say it doesn't matter,
come by the hammer,

toting the bucket,
board and nail,
it doesn't matter

what death does.
I say what I always say.
You were like a father.

Here

He slept in a closet in a room full
of the ground. He was a father.
His son went mooning after.

Ok, sky full of rain: I wept.
In maudlin England, where they keep
the metaphor for such things,

there was no more room, poor island,
for the laying-in. But I think
right here is room enough for all

of us. My father slept on a door for days
dreaming I would be back in time.
Nobody dies except he disappears.

We look all over the house for him.
Then we find the hole in a room.

Drunk

Once, in Canada, at dusk,
in the middle of a lake,
you stood up in the boat,
back to the sun,
a bottle of beer
in one hand,
your hat in the other,
and shouted at whatever rises,
whatever falls.

It was a poorman's summer.
I remember how
we rocked to the tune
of your voice on the water.
You wanted to dance,
you wanted to hug
your shadow.
In a cold country, nowhere,
you wanted to turn us over.

I was old enough to be afraid.
And some nights, still,
in the middle of sleep,
I hold my breath
as the bed drifts out
of its rocking dream:
I see you on the water,
nothing in your hands,
but dancing.

Counting Coup

Something like going back to second base
        to tag up.
    Your mother on the other end
of the phone
            crying: she wants to die,
like being on television forever.

*

Father, son, ghost. The third part
            is always a woman:
    a wife, like morning fog,
the mother of your children,
        who do not exist,
your mother, asleep in the next room.

*

Silence. A man is always coming home.
            He thought his father
    was the wrong god. His wives
marry other men,
        drift into daylight,
disappear. He marries again.

In Sleep

So finally you float to the surface
full of dead fish and the half-moon of a lung

and slowly, as in waking, you begin to open
all your body, bob, and with both hands
wipe the water clear

and with all your weight holding you up
at last you begin to see what it was

the earth drifting, your parents dead
and face down, drifting, like a bird
towing a wind

your sister, like the past of all flesh, drifting

and one wife, one wife, one wife
every one tied to the planet

all your dead drifting
the cloud of your body tied

but the blue eye of the earth
looking out

at silence
at the absence of earth

the moon
on the waters of your face
shining back at you

Summing Up

These now are the final figures of my father:
he lies in state in the long boat
of his own body
he is perfectly alone
his arms are tucked into a ceremony
of sleeves his face is soft
in its little anger
he looks like a governor

I have come back a thousand miles for this
in the next room the air is acrid
and stained as an attic window
I hardly recognize what I remember
this is Ohio it is two o'clock
a hand is raised and my mother blessed
she sits like his ghost
with his flower pinned to her breast

The End of the Indian Poems

The pony air, wild wheat.
Sun the length of its shadow everywhere.
Montana. Dakota.

I want to lie down.
In the middle of the day, among
these stones, I want to go to sleep.

The snowtracks that lead out of my body,
the pony-prints, the wind
hovering the pale grass . . .

I don't want to walk in the circle
of a bird over bones,
the Hawk That Hunts Walking,

I don't want to walk in the circle
of my name
anymore. I know where I am.

I know the moon has my face on it,
I know the leaves tremble
like a tree of fish—

I know that winter
is a white country, but I want
to lie down.

I want to lie down here,
among stone and sunlight,
on the buffalo ground, anywhere.

One of Us

Think about ten years ago
when loneliness was simply
lack of company,
or later,
when it was three-,

four-sided crowds,
parties in the morning,
or the other side, and
the politics of talk
was like applause

above silence.
I think about now:
about the quiet,
the dark, the hard edges,
the purity in single words,

the few friends, like physicians,
and the women,
for whom the body broke
like bread.
I think about now

the way one thinks
about the future,
how the mind, all alone,
makes it up in order to deal
with what is coming.

The Wish to Be a Red Indian

If one were only an Indian, instantly alert,
and on a racing horse, leaning against the
wind, kept on quivering jerkily over the
quivering ground, until one shed one's spurs,
for there needed no spurs, threw away the
reins, for there needed no reins, and hardly
saw that the land before one was smoothly shorn
heath when the horse's neck and head would be
already gone.

—Franz Kafka